Detective Work

Paul Broadbent

Contents

The Robbery

A robbery has taken place. This was the scene half an hour before the robbery. What time is it?

Point to the tallest thing in the yard. Then find the shortest thing.

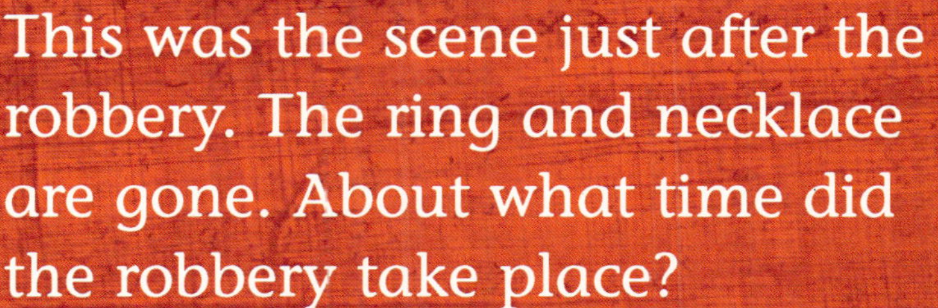

This was the scene just after the robbery. The ring and necklace are gone. About what time did the robbery take place?

Find 3 things that are the same and 3 things that are different in the two scenes.

o'clock

half past

quarter to

quarter past

Reporting the Crime

First, the crime needs to be reported to the police. Their phone number is 911. Do you know your phone number? Is it longer or shorter than this one?

The robbery took place on Thursday, June 8, at in the morning.

The owner was cleaning her jewelry in the backyard.

She went inside for 15 minutes.

An 8-inch (20-cm) necklace and a gold ring were stolen.

A police officer writes down all the details. How long is the necklace?

The time now is 11 o'clock. The police will arrive in half an hour. What time will it be?

If he is a quarter of an hour late, what time will he arrive?

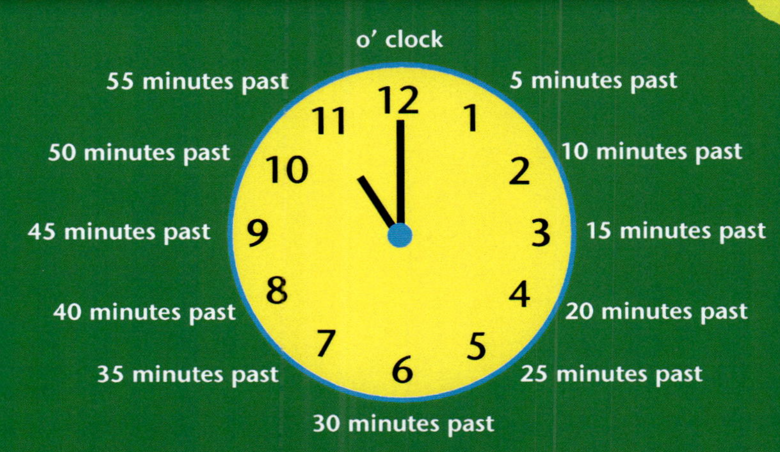

5

Police Officers

The police try to make sure that people obey the law. Some police officers work in stations. Others are out in cars, on bicycles, on foot, or even on horseback.

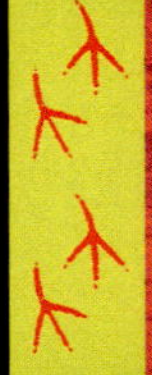

Which police officer is the tallest? Which is the shortest?

It used to be that police officers had to be a minimum height to join most police departments.

You can tell what kind of job a police officer does by the clothes he or she wears. Patrol officers wear a uniform. Detectives wear regular clothes.

Patrol officer

Detective

Police officers' hats come in different sizes. What size is M in inches? How many inches larger is XL than S?

Size	S	M	ML	L	XL
In.	20	21	22	23	24

Can you see a pattern in the inch sizes? Describe it.

Detectives

Detectives investigate crimes by looking for evidence and clues. Sometimes they measure things at the scene of a crime.

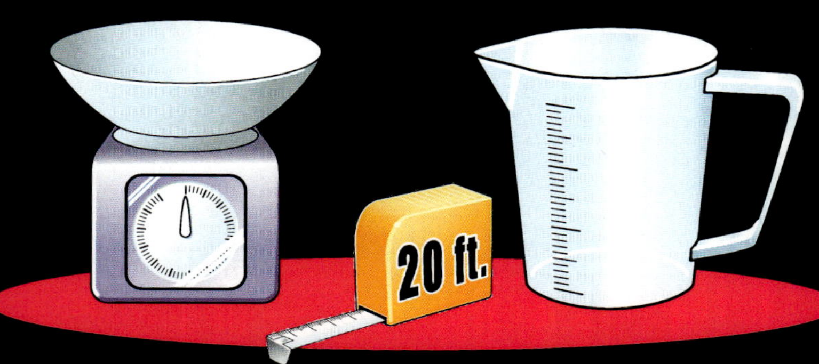

How could these measuring tools be used to take measurements of each item?

Packages

Glass of orange juice

Sherlock Holmes is a fictional detective who often uses a magnifying glass to find clues. A magnifying glass makes things appear larger.

Large footprint

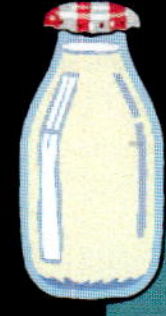
Bottle of milk

Tire tracks

Footprints are useful clues to see who was at the scene of a crime. Compare these footprints.

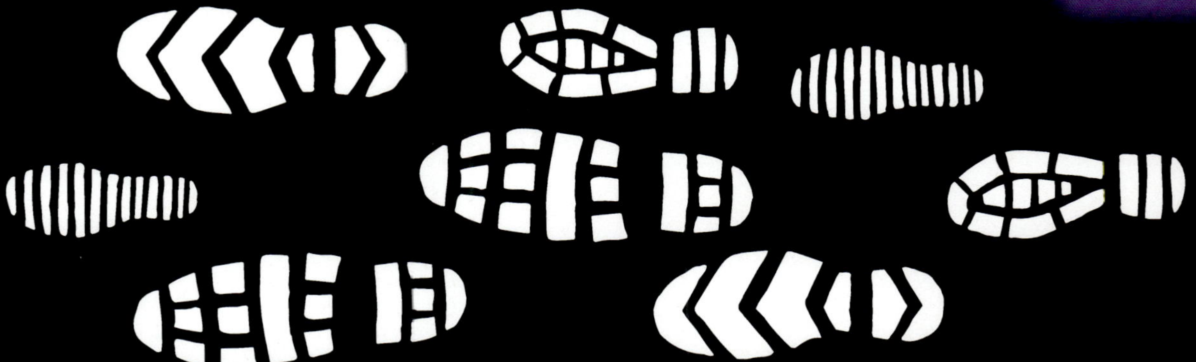

Which pairs go together? Which are the longest prints? Which are the shortest prints?

Match the shoes to the prints above.

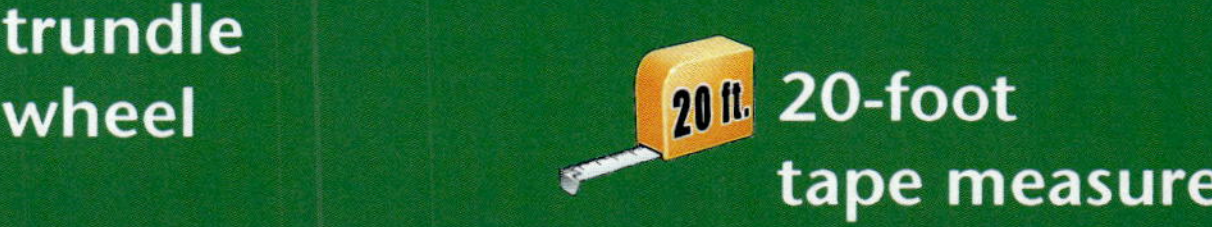

Looking for Clues

The detective measures the length of the fence by measuring it in paces. Each pace is about 3 feet (.91 m). The fence is about 12 feet (3.6 m) long.

How long is 1 of your paces?
Pace out the length of your classroom.

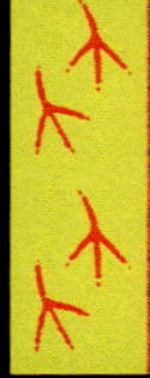

Near the fence, the detective finds two short footprints, a twig, a shiny candy wrapper, and a feather.

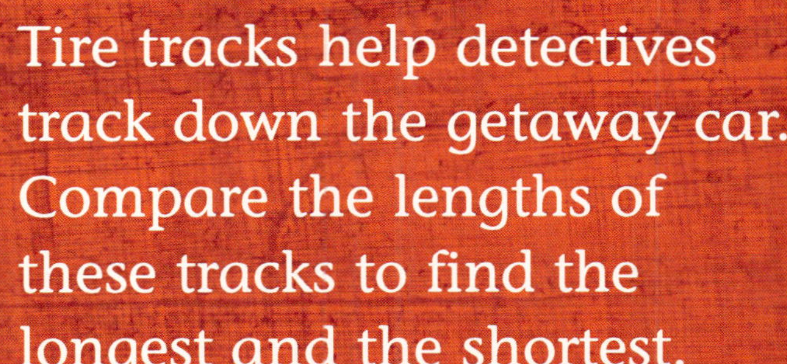

a

b

c

d

e

Estimate, then measure the length of each track in inches.

Put the tracks in order of length, starting with the shortest.

Prints

Fingerprints help detectives find people who were at the crime scene. The skin pattern on every person's fingers is different.

Compare these fingerprints. Describe them using math words.

This glass is almost empty. Someone has been drinking from it. How many fingerprints can you see?

- empty/full
- long/short
- curved/straight
- wide/narrow

Handprints are also used. Explain the difference between a hand print and a fingerprint.

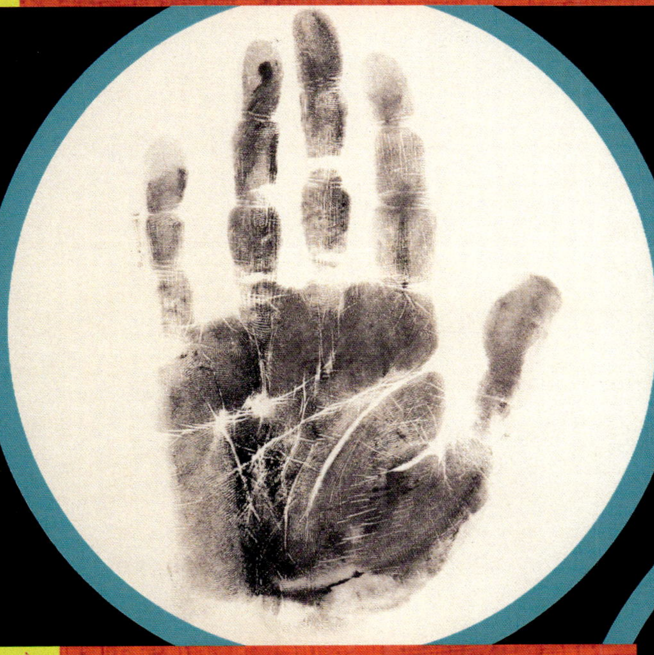

Compare these handprints. Which pinky finger is the longest?

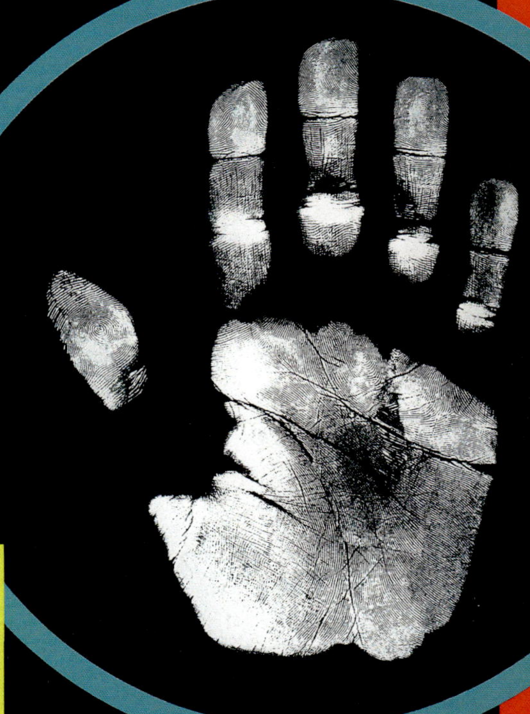

Use a ruler to measure the lengths of each of your fingers.

Picture Perfect

The police ask witnesses to describe people at the scene of the crime. Describe yourself using "measure" words.

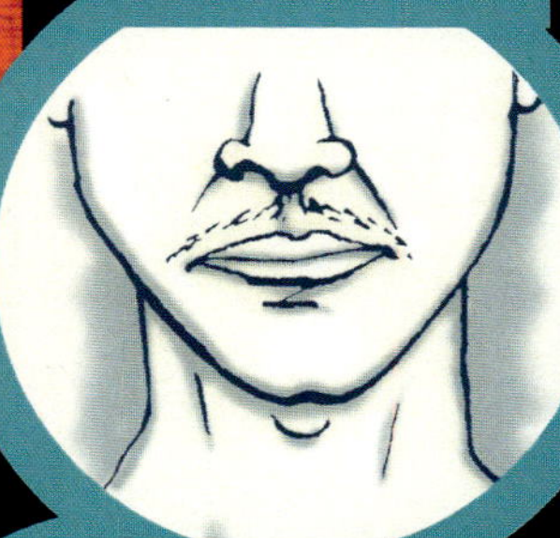

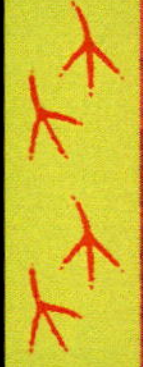

Match the pictures with the descriptions.

Computer software helps people build a lifelike picture from descriptions witnesses give.

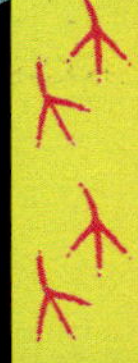

The software puts together these features to make a clear image.

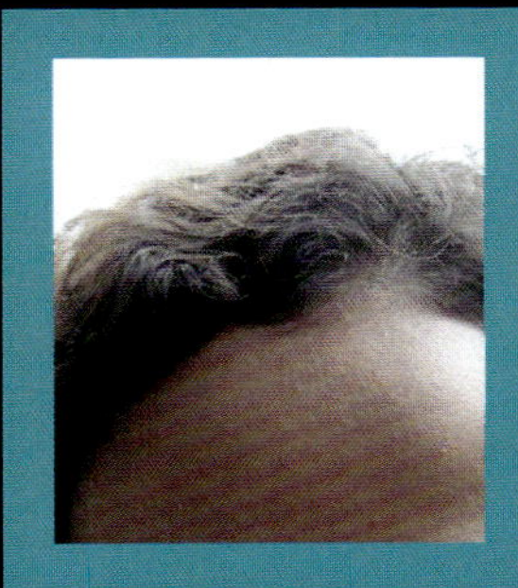 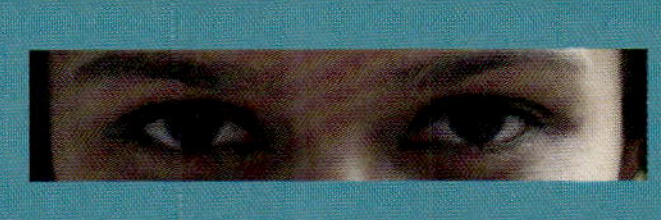 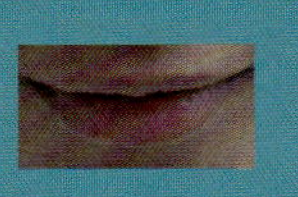 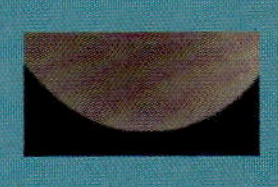 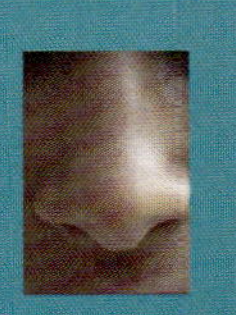

Describe the features using math words – what will the completed photo look like?

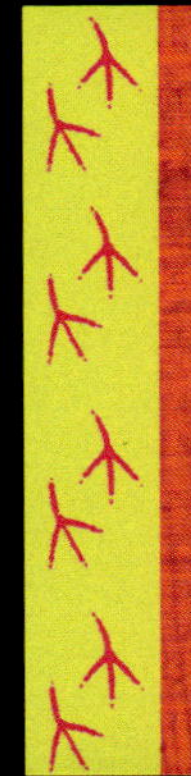

The detective decides which person the picture matches best. Who do you think is chosen?

Stolen Goods

People give descriptions of stolen goods to the police. Police officers then try to find these things.

Read these descriptions. Match them to the pictures.

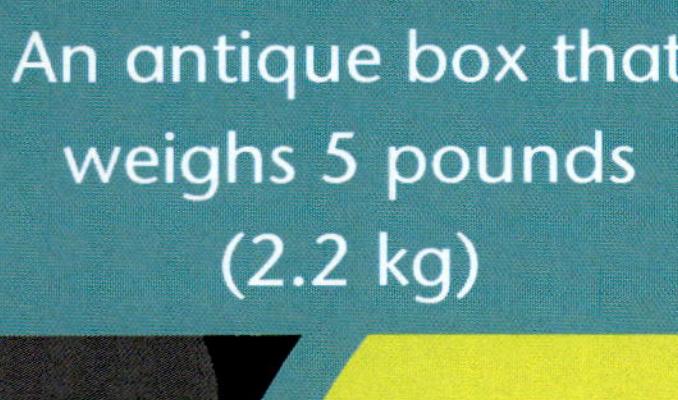

An antique box that weighs 5 pounds (2.2 kg)

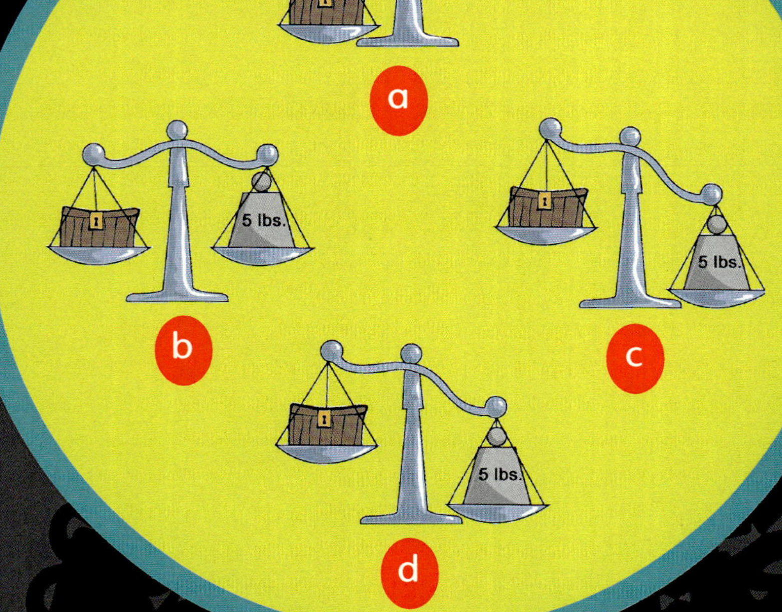

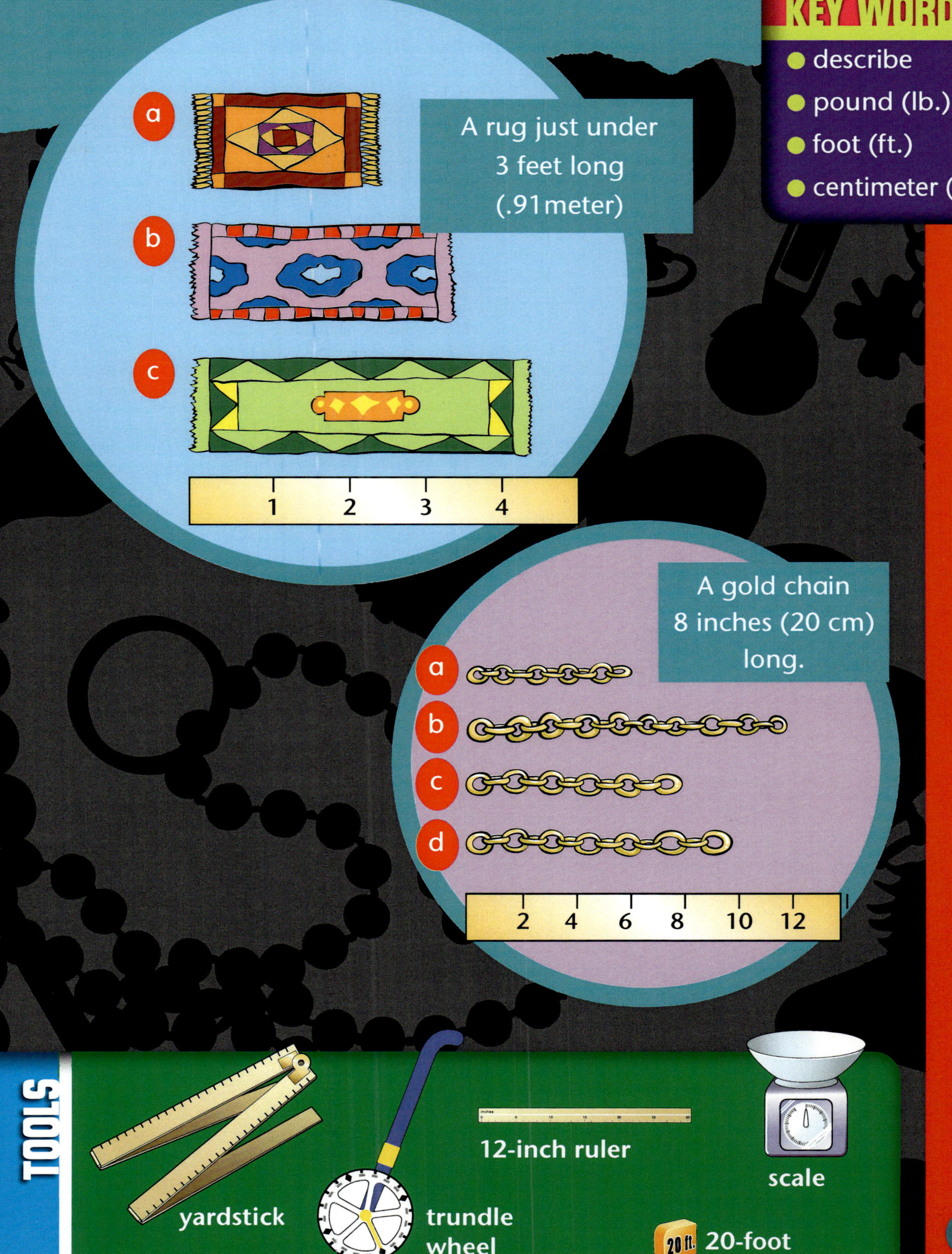

KEY WORDS
describe
pound (lb.)
foot (ft.)
centimeter (cm)

a

A rug just under
3 feet long
(.91 meter)

b

c

1   2   3   4

A gold chain
8 inches (20 cm)
long.

a
b
c
d

2   4   6   8   10   12

TOOLS

yardstick

trundle
wheel

12-inch ruler

scale

20 ft. 20-foot
tape measure

A Detective's Day

Detectives write down the things they do each day. Here are a detective's notes for 1 day. What did he do at 8 o'clock?

Morning

Early start
to clean out
some files

Checked
fingerprints
and pictures
of suspects

Interviewed
witnesses

When did the detective interview the witnesses?

The interviews took 2 hours. What time did they finish?

Afternoon

Drove to the crime scene

Looked for more evidence

Back to police station for a meeting

What happened at 2 o'clock?
How long was the detective doing this job?

He left the police station at 12 o'clock and returned at 5 o'clock. Count in hours to find how long he was gone.

TOOLS

7 o'clock

8 o'clock

9 o'clock

10 o'clock

11 o'clock

12 o'clock

19

Interviewing Suspects

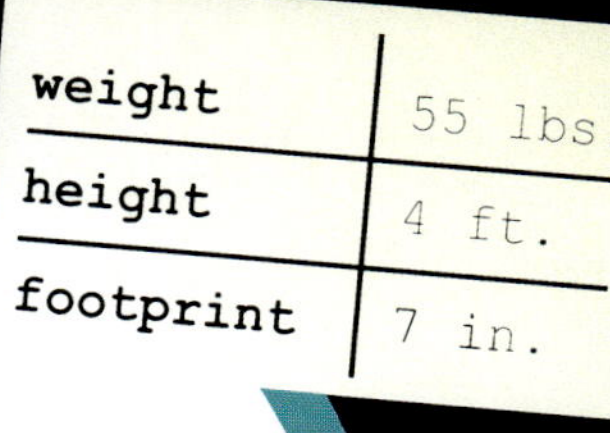

weight	55 lbs.
height	4 ft.
footprint	7 in.

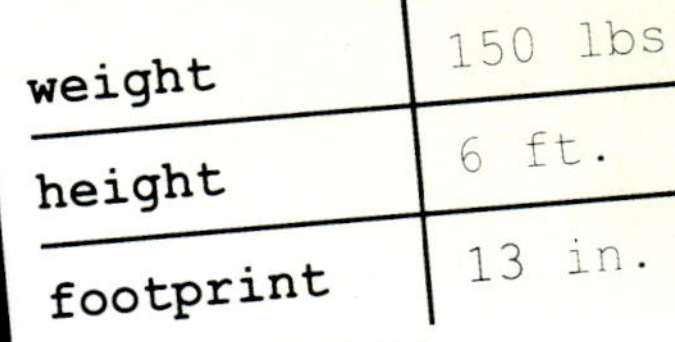

weight	150 lbs.
height	6 ft.
footprint	13 in.

Milkman

Young girl

weight	143 lbs.
height	5.5 ft.
footprint	11 in.

Letter carrier

Who is the tallest suspect?
Who weighs less than 60 pounds?
Whose footprint is 11 inches long?

The detective interviewed the 3 suspects about the missing jewelry. These are the notes he made:

Suspect	Evidence	Interview	Possible suspect?
A. Next-door neighbor (young girl)	• Small footprints • Candy wrapper	"I was playing with a light ball. The wind blew it over the fence. I climbed over and got the ball. I didn't eat any candy."	?
B. Letter carrier	• Footprints • Packages • There around the time of robbery	"I left two packages at about half past 10. The smaller one was heavy, more than 10 pounds (4.5 kg), and the larger package was light. I left them on the sidewalk by the gate."	?
C. Milkman	• Fingerprints • Milk bottles • There around the time of robbery	"I delivered a bottle of milk just before half past 10. My crate of bottles was heavy and I had to rest. It was sunny and birds were flying around, but there was nobody in the yard. I saw the jewelry but I didn't touch it."	?
D. Unknown	• Quick mover • Silent • Candy wrapper • Feather • Twig		?

Look back at the clues. Who do you think stole the jewelry?

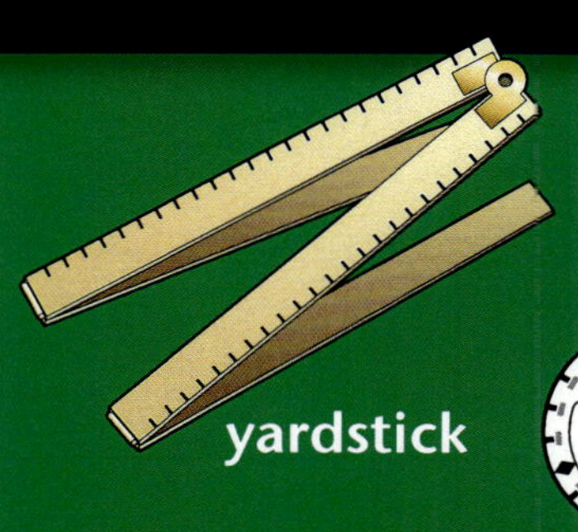

Solving the Crime

These are the clues found by the detective. Which clues did the detective need to measure the length of? Which clues gave information about the person?

Twig on ground

Shiny candy wrapper

Feather

Milk bottle

Small footprint

Packages

Side gate open

Large footprint

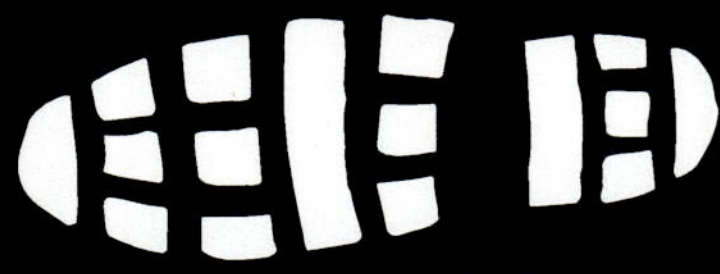

Tire tracks

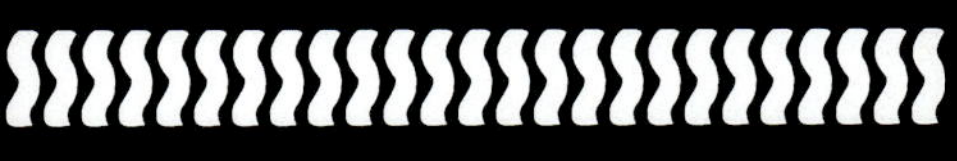

The detective put together all of this measuring evidence and solved the crime.

This shows what happened. Put these in order to find out how the jewelery was stolen.

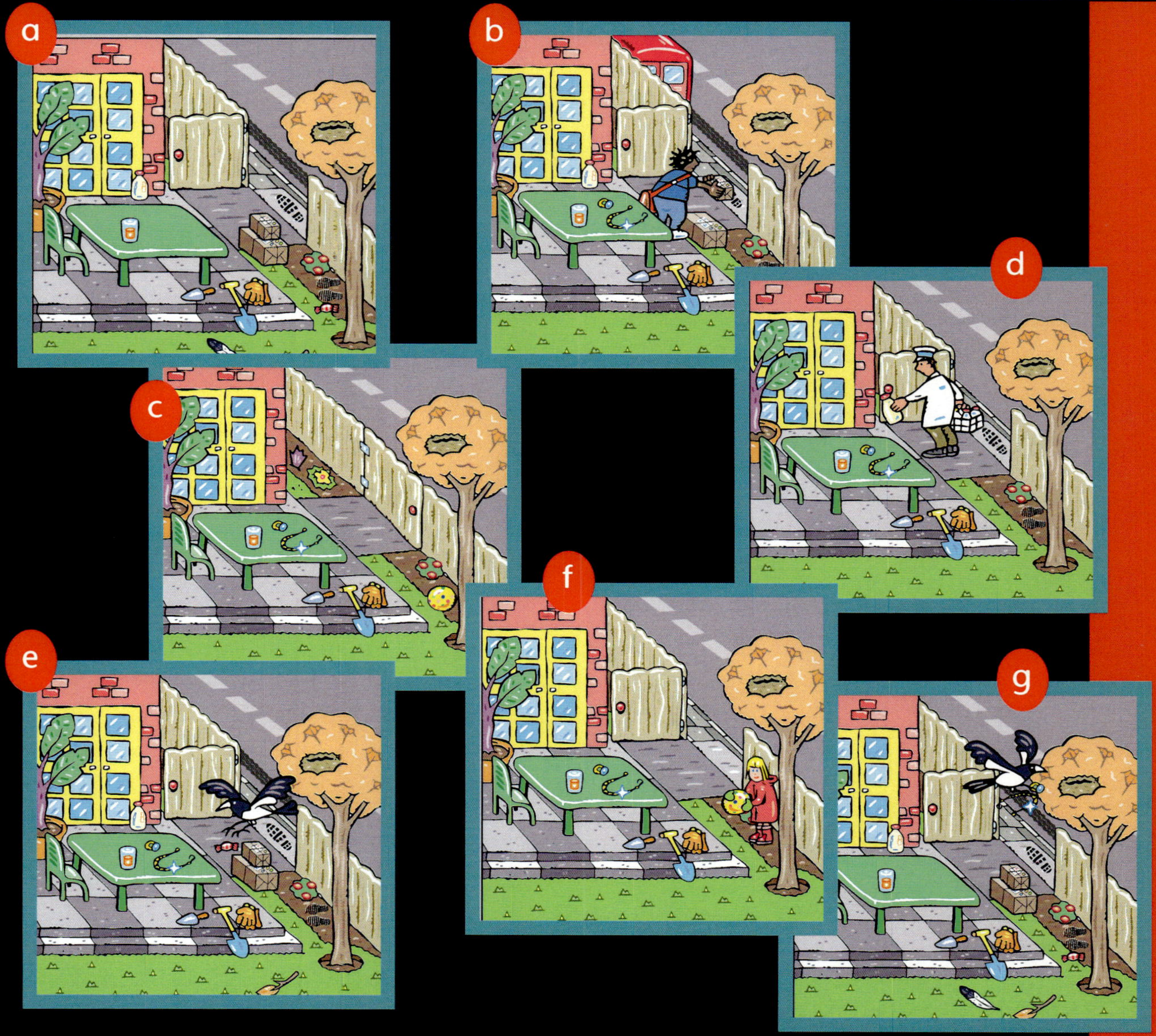

a

b

d

c

f

e

g

1st	2nd	3rd	4th	5th	6th	7th	8th	9th	10th
first	second	third	fourth	fifth	sixth	seventh	eighth	ninth	tenth

Sum It Up

What is the time on this clock?
What will the time be in 30 minutes?

Which is the longest chain?
Which is the shortest chain?
Put the chains in order of size,
starting with the shortest.

a 

b 

c 

d 

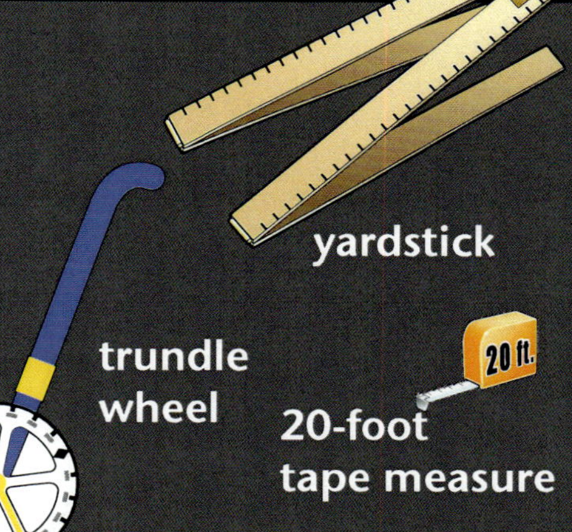

Which tool would you choose to measure the chains?